Praise for *& more black*

I'm so excited for t'ai freedom ford's silky, tough, clear-eyed, and irreverent new collection. These poems suffer none of the ongoing American foolishness. They snap so hard you might— as 1 did—jump up and run out of the room laughing at their brilliant, slicing wit. They are composed with soul and funk and lightning-fast intelligence. This poet will reward your reading over and over with her impressive power and relentlessly exuberant music. Read them aloud. *& more black* is truth moving at the speed of sound. —**Patrick Rosal**

& more black

t'ai freedom ford

Augury Books • New York

Contents

Darkness very dark darkness is sectional.

—Gertrude Stein

#notorious

who we be? you already know— must be
groovy & rhythmic   quixotic   erotic
exotic   ethnic   must be east indian
with all the red dots on our foreheads must be
picnic   pick a nigger   loop a noose round her neck

must be disrespectful   neck swivel & eye roll
pick & roll   basketball   our namesake
pump fake & fast break   must be breakfast   brown
thief   suddenly ground beef see how bullets
scramble legs   must be dangerous   jail cells

cannot contain us   tame us   us anger   shameless
thus anger hangs us   we be beautiful & blameless
hollywood shuffle   *nigger entertain us*   must be
tragic   traffic   target you don't know us
till triggers name us   murder us   we famous—

southside

shorty shine shonuff but she got issues
shellshocked from block showdowns   glocks
& shotguns   chiraq's finest   minus shrapnel & shit
she sh-clack clack   she boom shaka-laka
chakra sure shock   body rocker shonuff
seen nuff shenanigans   nuff knuckleheads
shackled & cuffed   she tough but smooth   shine
shonuff   all Vaseline & sheen   shinbones shimmering
sun be throwing shade on she brownskin parade
all shine & fine & shameless & nameless
in shit—i mean   who she be?   shapeshifting
landscapes   fire escape shoutout   she shimmy
shimmy yaw   shmoney honey   sugar in the raw
she shutdown suckas   shine   sure as she living

misguided little unforgivable hierarchies
after Wangechi Mutu

he who is grown wears the crown: gold: crooked
she who is grown wears the crowning glory:
old: naked: she who is grown wears the gown:
peplum of black nipples feathered waistbeads
he who is grown owns himself only owns
a bed of weeds only needs his shit as
fertilizer   she who has grown fertile
wears herself backbending atop herself
she who is grown wears the town: bold: church hat
balancing act—steeples peopled with light
threatening topple from nigger sky scrape
squat—motorcycle *vroom vroom* in poom-poom
baldheaded eyeballs kaleidoscope splotch—
she who is grown wears black (w)heels: knows her name.

root of all Eves

after Wangechi Mutu

her name mean *pornstar* in ebonics: fucks
flickering electric in whiteboy head
she made of paper; she tear easily
crumple in his palm like a mistake oops
origami pussy: now she a swan
he ruffle her feathers with his magic
wand blonde weave down to her ass crack apple
bottom of the barrel black blasphemous
she pre-Jesus—tongue embroidered with lies
little lacy things like doilies in shit
hell yeah he hit that then fucked up them pies
while she unfolded herself smoothing her
wrinkled eyes her prized thighs her right nipple
her other self buried brown sprouting roots

some said you were the spitting image of evil
after Carrie Mae Weems

you became drum became washboard became
hum became tincan became numb became
cowbell became screendoor became dirtfloor became
skillet became clothesline became dumb became
plow became yardbird became heifer & bitch became
wagon became hitch became bible became barbwire became
strum became headrag became drum became
biscuit became pitchfork became hum became
slopjar became shit became northstar became
pitstop became boxspring became mule became
numb became shotgun became sunflower became
battleaxe became dumb became whisper became

drum—

i sell the shadow to sustain the substance

after Glenn Ligon & Sojourner Truth

as black woman i am untitled—nameless
my heart   a faint glow of neon wire
buzzing toward some shameless demise
i stand against walls looking nonchalant
flashbulbs mistake me for celebrity
or   bored whore   same difference—as black woman
i am installation art as negress
my heart   a black plastic bag ghosting streets
what parts of we ain't for sale as woman?
black skin   shiny as gold teeth   worthless swag
is this body possible? or do i
merely exist as melancholy gesture—
self-portrait as shrug   eye roll   blank stare
sacrificing shadow   the body remains

The Rebirth or HeyGirlHey

after Alexandria Smith

what they don't tell you is the white picket
fence is splintered & weathered & tethered
to a mortgage—a death sentence of normal
your limbs taunt lawnmowers & anything
with teeth   you peel back pastel wallpaper
feed pasty strips to the flames whispering
in your closet—& so you die   come back
with too many mismatched legs & arms
all wanting to strangle you as you run
but see how smart you be? how you buried
your throat in them bushes of blackgirl hair—
how the clueless limbs wave: *heygirlhey*
what they won't tell you is the white picket
fence was once brown & dull just like your skin

Billie Holiday never met Miss Chiquita (Banana)

ghost rot & electrified warble in the wake
of Auto-Tune reek of something fraudulent:
egos without deodorant stinking like Lincoln's
legacy—some peg-legged freedom with gold
fronts stuntin' on this high-pitched peekaboo
slurring words that rhyme with rich—okeydoke
code switch conjugating *nigger* into *nigga* into
platinum: the past tense of penis   the square
root of chicken picnics   pictures all pink-gummed
& gingham   the old hunky dory story
of a world where we can't whistle without
digging up teeth to the tenth power—our smiles
a bouquet of flames for history's rotisserie

suite for a family displaced by fire
Astoria projects circa 1983

i. Mr. James

smoke be a sneaky motherfucker
it got no hands but hold you like a lover
seducing your lungs with its black   magic
poof! it make everythang disappear   wear
its black like a nightgown   all sexy in shit
midnight marauder   it take your breath away

smoke be a blindfold   make you use your hands
as eyes   everythang you grope   a prize
ski vest   rollerskates   Dog barking his face off
flame nowhere to be found   just the sound
of smoke   fucking your lady till her milky skin
ain't nothing but smudge   you move but don't budge
cause smoke stupids your feet   & outta nowhere heat
& flame   with her big-ass mouth   calling your name

ii. Michelle

projects ain't half bad   'cept they think my dad
crazy   he just a little hazy in the head
cause mommy dead   & brother don't talk much
he ain't dumb but fire twisted his throat to pretzel

kids round here don't ask bout our skin—the braids
of veins—the two-toned tightness of it   mostly
they in awe of the lightness of it   beach sand
brown   & our blonde curls   big girls turn to braids

least daddy got Dog but fire made him mean
he chase kids up the chainlink   chew at they Chucks
till dad call him off   feed him a piece of hot dog

in the dream: brother a superhero
got flames for wings   they betray him with strangle
still he struggle to name the no-name things

ii. brother

mommy used to let me light her cigarettes
on the stove so i wasn't afraid of flame
it was something i could turn on & off
tick tick tick   on & off   a heat i could tame
a twist of the wrist   a soft blue whisper
a hiss of gas   grows an orangey flame
at scouts we rubbed twigs   gathered sprigs & brush
& huffed & fussed for a measly flame

cigarettes are cool for making rings of smoke
but they sting your lungs & make you choke
matchsticks are magic   quick flickers of flame
& lighters are dumb   they listen to your thumb
but flame needy as a tongue   it knows your name
it licks your bones & devours your home

iv. Dog

i let the boy call me Dog cause i am
& what better they know   sleeping   house full
of so much smoke i can't track they scent
i follow the choke of them   get a chunk of him
then drag & drag till the air taste different
days later i go back—nose the ash & bone
of what used to be   paws caked with char
this what sadness smell like   i am called away

the new house smells old   bacon grease   cheap paint
but i ain't one to complain   plus there's a river
it shimmers in the sun   but stinks a little:
rusted metal   dead diapers   drowned squirrels—
what i miss most is her skin   not the scent
                    but the salt of it

v. Mommy

in the dream i am walking on hot coals
in the desert of my imagination
i am teetering on a tightrope of flame
my name is irrelevant in this hell
& what is that smell? a barbecue of flesh
my hair: a golden helmet of singe
i binge on a bathtub full of hot sauce

in the dream i'm sleeping on the sun's surface
a corona of flame serenades me
each little tongue a kiss of sweet blister
and there—Michael and his sister—at the door
glass figurines filled with blue-green water
they come closer but each step is a mistake
holograms of slosh & scream i cannot break

there ain't enough water for all of us

you could call it shade   a parade of salt
raining on your wounded retrograde   even
the planets imitate your backwardness
disco driftwood awkwardly afloat in a sea of super
model piss & trap boy spit—O! God! such sudden
glory leaves skin incandescent & flimsy:
a feast of raisins   & other filthy reasons
make throat carcasses   O'Keeffe canvasses on crack
Kanye landscapes of beige-brown-beige stage protests
of grotesque testicular proportions
your psychic warned you   this pastel hell   this
dust garden   succulents sucked dry & lustless
everything   a fucking mirage

20,000 leagues under the sea

of course   this fiction   some cousin to Truth
like Stereotype in his youth   minding
his business   gnawing on a chicken bone
till paparazzi show   flashes gnashing
their teeth at the Black of it   slackjawed gaze
yardbird carcasses for days   negro infinity
sudden shoeshine & bowtie dandy—postcard
infamy   picturesque picnic where fruit grew
grotesque   never mind them ghosts   jilting overlords
with overboard antics   spirit coastguard
ebb & flow of holla & hallelujah
hell you gon' do but pose   muddy up the print
there it is—all hoax & spit   dark with the smoke
of it—a portrait: faces of chuckle & choke

how do i live today, every   day?

by forgetting that i am going to die—
but there is this massive city of a ship
in the middle of an ocean of invisible ink
the water that won't turn cold   the teeth brushing
the bacteria percolating at the gumline
the bassline of this song in my head   this waistline
oozing outward   these inward thoughts rattling
battling for a seat on the subway   at the table
this able body   unwilling   lackadaisical
only my heart in a rush   racing toward
some nowhere   & sudden days in between
these are all the reminder i need without
your exaggerated fears   your easy bullets

either way, you'll be in a pool of something
after ruby onyinyechi amanze

swimming: where even the kisses smell like
doom   waiting   baiting your breath in fishnet
wading in a capful of rainfall so small
pinky toes cause capsize   meaning you tiny
like bullet   like pellet   like capsules of happy
the shrink worked   a bygone blink & look!   you
singing some sappy lovesong   brink of backstroke
such leisure this life sans seizure & lurch
boys in blue   birds   way they perch   way the shit
on us & say it's rain   send our mamas humming
random hymns   & why couldn't we swim?   our brown
bodies & chlorine water making a warm funky tea
a contagious soup   black limbs flailing with so much joy

the deluge

after Alexandria Smith

not water   not at first   but an ocean
of sloughed wallpaper   thought i was drowning
wasn't nothing but a sea of flowers
clowning to kill me   or oxygen suck
tsunami fuck or float   die   tread water
dead daughter   damp house of dark dismantle
which way them legs?   what we make of this wet?
sudden cacophony of arrhythmia
offbeat rearrange of alla your shit
what voodoo culprit   church of leopard print
conjure this purge?   surge of armchair & birdcage
& uncle's secrets   eyeless & all teeth   submerged
if this be verge of death   why my limbs insist on
air   instead of letting lies do they dying

instructions for a storm

after Amaryllis DeJesus Moleski

reign topless   grab ya crotch miss   clutch an amethyst
spear   wear a skirt of atmospheric pressure
invite lightning & a flock of lavender irises
batwings sing a chorus of third eyes shadowed
blue-brown   this the Nu Nile magic hour
how a blackgirl urge a powersurge outta gunpowder
our power be in the marrow   how our
grandmamas' bones could summon tomorrow's
sunshower   devour doubt & make magic
outta drought   pluck a guitar from the clouds
& get loud   all thunder in shit   is you wet yet?
or at least dizzy   forecast partly frizzy
for the fish fry   bitch been fly   i'll make it plain:
alchemy's the only currency now   make it rain

root of all Eves (alternate take)
after Wangechi Mutu

there: herself and the square root of herself
incubating just below the surface
her trachea tree bark dark   organic
her body: a panic of random hands
feet of motorcycles, tail of purple
feathers—a headdress of chaos and thorns
she teeters between celebrate and mourn
the left arm a trunk of flesh recently severed—
perhaps punishment for picking what felt
free and firm as a missing left breast
machete is a motherfucker when
wielded by an angry god or at least
that's what the legend will have us believe
god or man   cleave or cleft   what is left?   Eve

what i risk to walk in this world as my full human self

spotting   full on bloodletting   wearing white   off
white   teeth   flinching at the sight of rice   kitchen
those shadowy curls at the nape   what only
a black girl know   humidity   at the risk
of sounding stupid   sanctuary   mud
in the forecast   scam: blackface   pocketful
of wild turkey   monkey on my back   throat
way the words curdle & return   call forth
& mimic   symmetry   wine watered down
to something syrupy   strawberry red
a familiar kool-aid   dance panic   boogey
resurrect   body non-cooperative
but body   nonetheless   just lesser—   & more black

Folie à Deux

after Alexandria Smith

put black girl hair under a microscope
& see space—a galaxy of naps seeking
light—here: we twin ourselves into beings
Siamese psychosis   a hocus-pocus of limbs
zigzag of woodgrain vertebrae   floating
universe   we solstice toward void shine
toward whiteness   toward bloodline whittled whack
think how black vacuum consumes   takes back our we

oh dark continent of kink   pink kneecaps
mutate two stages beyond beige   yonder
brown legs long to tapdance for an audience
of stardust   shuffle along & Sambo
that constellation of teeth   on the cusp of Tom—
oh Uncle, what dilemma this nappy hair
                                        —that white white arm

instructions for a freedom
after Amaryllis DeJesus Moleski

fuck flux: this universe tryna render you
redundant   a mere speck amidst the spectacle
of space   an unremarkable black hole
a dust bowl of nappiness   imploding whirlpool
of blackgirl cool   slave to sameness   spectrum
of humdrum   radioactive violence   disguised
as incomplete science   suckas solving for X
nevermind you lightyears beyond celestial
conspiracy   extraterrestrial delivery   dang!
you big bang in shit   cosmic   prehistoric
relics like bones & axes   retrograding
backwards   shooting stars ain't nothing but black
chicks doing back flips   fuck flux: gravitate
black & rotate that axis till this universe
                (((collapses)))

when work becomes werk

sitting in the exit row compels me
to halfway pay attention to the safety spiel
but the house music in my headphones renders
the message to choreography—a dance
of pointed fingers   arms extending & retracting
elbows tucked   & i think *we are fucked* cuz
the flight attendant is vogueing in sync
to the thump & hiss of bass & treble
troubling my ears   but she betta werk
that oxygen mask & fast hand geometry
femme realness giving me all kinds of life
until it ends & we taxi & ascend
doing that turbulence dance   a grateful boogie
& prayer to the sky gods for letting us
                 feel fly—

to the white man next to me texting the entire flight

ain't that the point?   to always be the exception
without being exceptional   to smoke the joint
but not inhale   to pale in comparison
to redden but not bleed   to flail but not get shot
to drive   to walk   to talk out the side of your
mouth   to be in the south & be safe   to pick
up your child   to pull out your license   to smoke
a cigarette in your car   to go to a pool party
to swim in a pool of your choice   that is not
your own blood   to voice your irritation
to play your music   loud   to be loud   to remain
silent   to need help   to give help   to have
the whole damn plane at the mercy of your fingertips

dance dance revolution

they don't dance no mo',
all they do is this —OutKast

it *is* movement: a hyper spasmic stutter
perhaps orgasmic or ecstatic in its locus
at once reckless & focused on the downbeat
the ghost note   the afterclap   sorta slapstick
in its looseness   all gumby on the drumbeat

a voyeuristic joystick   watching bombs tick
the strobelight fantastic   at once elastic
& rigid   perhaps robotic   (but not that cool)
foolish imitation maybe   so much math
in that choreograph   dancefloor long division

beer slosh remainder   flailing pale   eyeless
hands & hips all thrust in the hardwood darkness
trusting no rhythm save failing syncopation
& this how we get got   mesmerized by
the offbeat—

13 ways of looking at gentrification
after Wanda Coleman, Patricia Smith, and Letta Neely

a hipster, hip-hopper and broken hip walk into
a bodega— kombucha grape Snapple   Similac
for the grandbaby debit card   EBT card   WIC—
asymmetrical blue bob   a dark Caesar   a church hat
with a mean lean—coffee shop   barbershop storefront church—
obamacare   idontcare   medicare   *praise jesus*—
dollarsign   signofthetimes   sign on the dotted line
out of your mind   welfare line/chalk outline   out of time
brownstone   brownskin woes   coffee brown support pantyhose
potted plants stoop bliss   stopped & frisked   stop the madness miss
reality TV   reality: NYPD
but is the hood really "the hood" when white boy jogging
shirtless down Marcus Garvey?— *praise jesus   nigga please*

windows are the eyes to the soul

across the way the white people have moved
in—their windows golden like the glow of Jesus
& ain't this moment holy?   unpacking
shiny relics that emerge as if reborn
from dismantled boxes & gobs of newspaper

the fresh paint reeks of off-white   the newness
of things to come—sex   & of course babies
to fill the new rooms with their own little
messiahs   cries & sighs   soft against
the off-white beauty   & of course   equity

the newness of things to come like summer
& sirens   & brown bodies stacked on stoops
& church bells & hellish heat   & of course
electricity—the off-white air conditioner
humming like Jesus—i will pray for them

futureblack

circa 1983

us badass kids had the block on lockdown
spit burst from lips pursed   bathroom acoustics
ruthless beatbox   sound drowning out heartbeats
we started beats on dull lunchroom tables
amazed at how brown knuckles enabled
such sudden percussion—*kaboom boom bip*
kaboom bip—doomed hips with no choice but swivel
so Black & so brilliant   white boys shriveled
down to molecules   tryna be down with our cool
by osmosis   planet rock   hocus-pocus
them project bricks never broke us   only made us
more focused   wildstyle   we hopped turnstiles   fuck
ya tokens   us kids tough   rocked scuffed shelltoes
just broken in from breaking and striking poses—
                (& you know this)

transcript of an MTA audition

i sit wide-legged & grab my crotch
i sit wide-legged & adjust my nuts
i sit wide-legged & shift my dick two millimeters to the left
i sit wide-legged & scratch my balls
i sit wide-legged & consider the weight of my nutsack
i sit wide-legged & cup my nutsack
i sit wide-legged & estimate my nutsack weighs about five ounces
i sit wide-legged & hold my dick like a gun
i sit wide-legged & aim my dick at that chick over there
i sit wide-legged & pull the trigger
i sit wide-legged & murder these hoes
i sit wide-legged & smell my trigger finger
i sit wide-legged & slouch & side-eye whoever dares to watch

self-portrait as gay man

i'd conjure Basquiat—brown skin, paint flecked
hair: a curious matted sculpture of dust
salt water   feathers   sand   aloe   gold leaf
body: impossibly lean but not starved
ambitious maybe   vegan probably
i'd topple out of bars   bum cigarettes
not to smoke so much as smolder—watch white
boys watch my lips wrap around small white things
to them i am hip-hop: not Kanye   not even
Kanye's alter ego all soft speech & code switch
i'ma Kanye album to get fucked & fucked up to
some beautiful dark twisted fantasy
but i am more James Brown swag than Kanye shrug
hips: a funky drummer   the big payback

the distance between what we have and what we want
after Tavares Strachan

chicken anguish   chickenhead language   lost in
translation: Ebonics   Spanglish   pig latin
juke joint conjugation   *what it do*   *what it be*
what it was   lackluster   fuzzbuster   busted
stereotype hype: teeth vs beef   tooth vs
truth   *all that glitters*   something like sequins
weekend heathens   with ashy knees drawn to Jesus
praise be   to the lords of underground
that raised me   in the indigo weed haze
in my negrodian naivete   the white gaze
never phased me   but skittish with skittles
i skedaddle   straddle life & breath   battle
death rays aiming to amaze me   immortal
nothing & errythang twirl: the do or die portal

roadkill

oh deer, i am sorry for your roadside
funeral—speeding procession of shock & pity
we wonder how a deer dies—suicide?
& what of the fender that did you in
eyeless bastard with no regard for nature
this your backyard—black boys sympathetic though
know what it like to lie in the road for hours
the sun making fun of your composure
oh deer, how you decompose   bloodless body
party of rigor mortis   only your head
disintegrates into a mulch of leaves
black boys not as graceful   their clumsy blood
shimmers & shames the pavement   oh dear deer,
at least your death accident   though some'll say
                    you had it coming

Saul Williams could never be Miles Davis (no shade)

maybe in a movie with an 8-track soundtrack
flickering black in the back of his nappy skull
maybe if he imitated a lightbulb wearing a kilt
you know like green with brilliance but black
as Irish coffee the color of Pearl Cleage's milky
way maybe maybe maybe maybe maybe times
infinity is greater than or equal to the possibility
of square   minus hip to be   minus cocaine sinuses
minus the blackness of science   minus the science
of whiteness numbing my skull dull— maybe
if we squint   or duct tape   or say shit is soft serve
& maybe we deserve the worst kinda hero anyway
who turns his back on us   & blows   & blows

if someone should take your picture & make you black
for Aunjanue

remember when r&b singers were all
the rage & all the rage was trademarked Black
& Mary J. Blige wailed coked-up love songs
& Oprah was king of every little black
box inside whitefolks minds & whitefolks
minds wasn't nothing but a pancake box
of stereotype & Al B. Sure!'s lightskinned
voice pimped the airwaves—& then came Wesley
black & smooth as all our scars we thought ugly
& Halle quit David Justice & no justice no
peace—but that nigga Rodney was already
drunk off the settlement & celebrity
& yes—mediocrity is a motherfucker
although you'd never say it like that   still

i understand how tiring it is   the way rage
bubbles like a pot of grits   except ain't
no Al Green or any other reverend
to receive your holy metaphors & you are
better for it   & the world is better
because you present like Christmas morning
& Aretha's gospel ain't nothing but black
magic in the way that flour & water
& fatback make gravy   in the way we
die broke & indebted with nothing
for family to inherit but our gifts
blood-borne & cosmic & illegitimate
& inexplicable as any bastard—black
as any mirror staring back at us
                        with our own eyes

also known as fly nigga factory
after Erykah Badu

philosophy of finna   fish dinner Tuesday audacity
of ain't—praise this day we ain't bruised   ain't make
the news   hallelujah holiday   about-face them suede shoe blues
this the getdown   trajectory of come-up   colored section
inflection—epitome of hook-up   imagination of skillet
fried whitings & whitebread greasy as your nappy head
even our heart attacks operatic— where the peach tree be?
where your alcoholic uncle rocking ruffles & church shoes?
ain't he fly? don't he contain multitudes like your grandmama
pocketbook? fuck we made of 'cept peppermint, Vaseline
masking tape, butterscotch— assembly line of crunk   minus
punk-ass appropriation   funk soliloquy   cornbraids & cornbread
sardines & saltines   puttin' on the ritz   speaking of crackers—

ain't

suddenly these poems bore me these sentences
this syntax   these lines fragments   wagging they fingers

at me   this ironic ebonics   this king's English
bastard cockney bores me   these knock-kneed line breaks

this rhyme: internal   identical   metrical
Shakespearean especially boring   whoring

some eternal infamy   bores me   surely this
diction   these dictionaries   we call brains   call tongues

call mother   these similes   ain't bulletproof   niggas
still dead as dead niggas   still black niggas as black

as black is—   this bores me snores me to sleep   but sleep
is not dead   *amen*   i wake up but this woke bores me

this writing   this documenting   this archiving
this truthtelling   this shaming the devil   this

publishing (exclusive or nah)   ain't a cloak   ain't

a savior   (jesus or otherwise)   ain't a time

machine threatening reverse   ain't a nurse   ain't
a witch   ain't no magical stitch to hem up all them

wounds—   boring   every TV's blackface laughing at me
bores me   this prosody   this scansion   these lyrical

miracles glowed up on the page   ain't a suicide
bomb   ain't blowed up nothing corporate   ain't fed nobody

hungry   ain't nothing but a happy meal trap anthem
for the whiteboy singalong   they mouths all neon coil

these rhythms all African   these stanzas all white
& gaping   this shiny MFA thesis   this poet

laureate lux   this Pulitzer bling   this Pushcart
hustle   this blacktie book award ain't nothing

but a funeral   a hymn   a dirge   a eulogy

an apology   an afterthought so boring

i could cry   could fuck   could boogie   could whiskey
could die right fucking here could die could die could die

could die could die could die could die— bored AF &
waiting for these promising poems   these

impressive missives   these polished sonnets to save me
to give me my entire life   to be bread & wine

loaves & fishes   manna & mango nectar but
they ain't ain't ain't ain't ain't a sledgehammer   ain't

a deliverance   ain't a resurrection   a rewind
button   a second thought   a benefit of the doubt

ain't— ain't— ain't shit   but words shined to a sequined shimmy
now gimme my fucking fellowship   my POC retreat

my space amongst the trees   my university
position   my cup runneth over   ain't nothing

        to see here—

acknowledgments

9 poems from this book appear in a chaplet also entitled *& more black*, published by Belladonna*, Fall 2016.

'Preciate the dope-ass folks at the dope-ass literary places who made space for the following poems:

Apogee Journal: "Folie à Deux"

Beltway Poetry Quarterly: "either way you'll be in a pool of something," "what i risk to walk in this world as my full human self"

Eleven Eleven: "root of all Eves," "The Rebirth or HeyGirlHey"

The Feminist Wire: "i sell the shadow to sustain the substance," "some said you were the spitting image of evil," and "root of all Eves (alternate take)"

Gulf Coast: "Billie Holiday never met Miss Chiquita (Banana)"

The Lifted Brow: "instructions for a storm," "instructions for a freedom"

Muzzle Mag: "self-portrait as gay man"

Nepantla Anthology: "transcript of an MTA audition"

OCHO: A Journal of Queer Arts: "when work becomes werk"

RHINO Poetry: "southside"

The Rumpus: "ain't"

Southern Humanities Review: "the deluge"

Tin House: "Saul Williams could never be Miles Davis (no shade)"

Tupelo Quarterly: "roadkill"

Love to all my muses & teachers who appear within and without these pages: Tiffany Lina Alston, ruby onyinyechi amanze, Erykah Badu, Jean-Michel Basquiat, Christa Bell, Beyoncé, BLACK FOLK, Sandra Bland, Mark Bradford, Mahogany L. Browne, Wanda Coleman, Aunjanue Ellis, Ellen Gallagher, Erica Garner (rest in power), Terrance Hayes, Zora Neale Hurston, Arthur Jafa, Rashid Johnson, Glenn Kaino, Kanye (old & new), Glenn Ligon, Ryan McGinley, Amaryllis DeJesus Moleski, Saretta Morgan, Wangechi Mutu, Letta Neely, Frida Orupabo, Adrian Piper, Patrick Rosal, Jacolby Satterwhite, Alexandria Smith, Patricia Smith, Solange, Tavares Strachan, Sojourner Truth, Kara Walker, Carrie Mae Weems.

About the Author

& more black by **t'ai freedom ford** is a collection of what ford calls "Black-ass sonnets," which take their cues from Wanda Coleman's "American sonnets." For ford, the word "American" conjures the spirit of her ancestors. The poems are rebellious, outspoken, and take no shit. They investigate Black art, Black bodies, Black sexuality, and Black language, unapologetically and with a capital B.

Praise for *& more black*

& more black is full of "dance floor long division," Hello Kitty lunchboxes, double-dutch, and "dyke dowry." It remixes the visions and vernaculars of Wangechi Mutu, Amiri Baraka, Erykah Badu, Glenn Ligon, and countless others. It finds the music in Graceland quicksand and "Kanye's alter ego." "we be makeshift / bodies got too many mouths" t'ai freedom ford writes in these propulsive, poly-vocal, poly-verbal gems. This is a book holding spectacular spells, songs, and instructions for freedom. —**Terrance Hayes**

& more black
t'ai freedom ford

Augury Books • New York

& more black © 2019 by t'ai freedom ford

ISBN-13: 978-0-9995012-1-4

Cover design by Chiara Bartlett
Interior design by Shanna Compton
Edited by Kate Angus

Cover art by Alexandria Smith. Painting: *The Skin We Speak* (2017), 60" × 84" /
5' × 7', acrylic, oil, enamel on canvas; drawing: *the skin we speak* (2018), 11" × 15",
pen and marker on paper.

Published in the United States of America by:

Augury Books
154 N 9th St #1
Brooklyn, NY 11249
www.AuguryBooks.com
info@augurybooks.com

Distributed to the trade by Small Press Distribution (SPD)
www.spdbooks.org

Library of Congress Control Number: 2019930313

First Edition

Contents

When you removed the gag that was keeping
these black mouths shut, what were you hoping for?
That they would sing your praises?

—John-Paul Sartre, *Black Orpheus*

from here i saw what happened and i cried
after Carrie Mae Weems

the blood is red the blues is red the blues
is blood the red is dirt the dirt is brown

the brown is red the dirt is blood the blood
is blues the blues is brown the brown is skin

the skin is blood the blood is kin the kin
is red the red is blood the blood is new

the new is skin the skin is news the news
is brown the brown is noose the noose is red

the red is blues the blues is dirt the dirt
is skin the skin is blues the blues is kin

the kin is brown the brown is blood the blood
is news the news is black the black is new

the new is red the red is noose the noose
is black is blues is brown is red is blood—

people in glass towers should not imagine us
after Wangechi Mutu

i spy dark things dancing in my periphery

                i cross the street but it is only the trees

poplocking in the wind—my knees are dark things

        they click like triggers when i walk i fail

to notice sudden flinching—my body's

                post traumatic—i hail from dark things unknown

& cosmic   or, less romantic: niggerish

          & bionic like bullets arcing in the night

sky aching for other dark things to slow

             their trajectory—i fear these dark things

will be the death of me   reeking of Wednesday's

        blood & bourbon & bathroom reckoning

i pull dark things from the center of me

             & flush before considering their resemblance

cravings

if the chocolate is good it will melt

like a good lover darkens herself into

your sheets & disappears in a puddle

of moans—you will understand the science

of her invisible body but not

the fiction of her pulling you toward

some bloody orbit you do not crave—

this monthly reminder you are woman

in spite of wingtips & bowties you rock

estrogen is a catty bitch scratching

at your womb—an eyeless hag seeking sperm

& purpose beyond where eggs go to die

your body craving synchronicity

copycats your lover's fertility—

its false alarm

riding death in my sleep
after Wangechi Mutu

except i am awake   or so i think

my crotch—nothing more than a saddle
for her to climb atop & giddyup
black beauty thoroughbred: watch me gallop
find my stride in a field of daffodils
wet pussy   honeysuckle   i am all
muscle & rhythm—a sped-up heartbeat
verging collapse like a clapboard house
with too much wind   but we can't stop   won't stop
abdominal ache & grind   slick   bound by sweat
& other wetness   even her moans drip
with something sticky—a sap of sorts   spit?
shit: eyes closed we witness this murderous ride

i think: *goddamn   this   woman   could   kill   me*

you are a remarkable woman (now hurry up & die)
after Kara Walker

together they gathered the weapons
& placed them into baskets like fruits

their calloused fingers nimble & careful
the weapons otherwise questionable—

a hot comb   brick   a covered pot of grits
a spade clumped with soil   a soup ladle

a few choice shards from a broken teacup
a horseshoe   a small cast iron skillet

that smelled of cornmeal & burnt butter
the men   predictably   had already

removed real munitions from the big house
leaving nigger wenches to fend for themselves—

hardly defenseless after all they had
no panties & pounds of black pussy

> "Just because you love black pussy don't
> mean you love Black lives."
> —*Erica Garner @ Mayor Bill de Blasio*

sometimes the music starts playing unprompted & logical
people talking bout electrical shortages & i be talking bout
spirits & they demands   the need for song   & which song
was playing when you fell in love with her? was it something

easy & pleasing to the both of you—like Stevie—something
white folks have learned to love—& was she just another lesson?
a dark deep variation on a theme?   did gospel music swell
in the background? did the bed quake in the wake of some hallelujah

chorus—her pussy a forest of light   did you leave feeling
anointed?   holy?   across the street the Spanish church
is alive with cowbell & clave   but this life here ain't no religious
experience—tell me, when she said: *i do*   were you born

again?   would you have been just an average savage
                                        without her?

14

with that ass, they won't look at your eyes
after Mark Bradford

because eventually everything is reduced
to abstraction like too loud song becoming
a blues note—a footnote for the news—then static

      then dynamic because eventually everything
      is reduced abstract like blackness becomes black
      caricature like a too tight glove   courtroom antics

cue the greek chorus of anti-semitic semantics
because eventually everything is re-juiced
electrified abs track & field niggers high jump

      while black blurs master hurdles   did massa say
      how high / how feet / how knuckle/ how buttock / how thigh
      become bluestreak / how running while black becomes

literal not abstract like running for hobby
pale knobby knees   literal like bullet   then blurrr—
      —then static

the pornography store is closed so you
will have to make your own death

turn off the news— unless, the news turns you on
all that flesh & blood   blacking up the screen   mute
button scream   police ticker tape parade   quiet
riot in these streets   or, is it all a graveyard of boulevards
walking dead   zombie apocalypse ain't got shit on us
turn off the news— unless, the news is your turn-up

---

niggerskin glistening & confettied like dismal disco balls

---

we the latest dance craze: *the whip   the playdead   the chokehold*
the taser   cousin to *electric boogaloo*   but less animated
this dying   like lynching but less antiquated   blood
the new black   turn off the news—   but fuck   radio bleeding too
just more metaphor   karma pharmaceutical   the needle
you need   a shot in the arm   that dope   shit

badass

after he died, me & Gil Scott had dinner
some dingy diner Uptown where cabbies
came for coffee between shifts—he ate soft
boiled eggs cause it was easier to get down
since smack had snatched his front teeth & his mouth
was a graveyard of decaying brown stumps
other than that   he looked good   considering

he asked me bout my writing   told him all my poems
had bullets in them   he changed the subject
told me bout a yoga class he & Amiri took
where they had to balance banned books on they heads
& how the books were heavy & made him angry
& when he laughed   the hooks in his head made him ugly
& how they promised him new teeth after a year of good
          behavior

ancestors

both granny & papa, or at least the dust
of what's left of them, lie in unmarked graves
barely buried   funerals become makeshift
family reunions   fashions shows of fried chicken
& borrowed suits   paper plates & collection
plates cause don't matter who died   preacher gets paid
while we get drunk or high   or swole on sweet potato pie
& i am ashamed   not of my broke(n) ass
family but of myself for not knowing
where i might rip overgrown weeds from stubborn
roots—where i might place these wilting white lilies
why   amidst all these stony names   does the dirt
all look the same   & how many times have i
earned the chiseled cement to set them apart

everything out our mouth magic

we was born year of the boogie: 73
a brand new heavy   mouthful of feathers
& tar & guitar   we was fly collar blue
black   descendants of the letter R
rhyme with *horror*   got ghosts up in our throats
they background sang gravy & twang on the boogie
that thang they couldn't name   a mystery
in our cotton mouths   bastard of so many souths
& saltwalter & such   &   the too much
what we spoke   broken   we be makeshift
bodies got too many mouths   hear how we walk
what better we know   but it lookded good
we don't remember what we remember
but damn if tongue don't be   an heirloom

in America even the black sheep are white

my mouth is a museum of moving
images   ignorance is this nigger & his twitter
scrimmages   motherfucker i'm bionic
check the tonic in my lineage   her spine
an abacus of dreams   my fingers count
the cartilage between disenfranchised
& privileged   we be the in between
squishy & niggerish   indigenous
with heathenish tendencies   sacrilege
black power packages   bridge kunta
kinte to white christmases   what sort of
gift is this   i make gibberish of English
nasty as black licorice   we don't tapdance
no more all we do is this: (middle finger
                                    emoji)

self-portrait exaggerating my black features

after Glenn Ligon & Adrian Piper

my hair be a graveyard of black fist picks
my hair be a locked bag of magic tricks

my eyes be like two machetes shining
my eyes be like cosmic stars divining

my nose be like a magnolia tree
my nose be like Harriet black & free

my nostrils be flared toward yardbird perfume
my nostrils be aware of tree root's doom

my mouth be like Malcolm at the window
my mouth be like a weeping willow

my teeth be a full clip of hollow points
my teeth be like arrows with sharpened points

my tongue be a tambourine rattling
my tongue be a house nigga tattling

self-portrait exaggerating my white features
after Glenn Ligon

don't my sentences end up like questions?

   ain't these blonde hairs on my forearm pretty?

don't my small mouth rattle off suggestions?

   ain't my skin sunburnt, attitude shitty?

don't my eyes glow light brown in the sunlight?

   ain't the bottoms of my feet light skinded?

don't my brand of skinny incite gunfights?

   ain't my life where black boys began? ended?

don't my fine aesthetic dictate fashion?

   ain't my facial expression self-entitled?

don't my family tree pale in comparison?

   ain't my pedestal high & unrivaled?

   ain't my nose all narrow & aquiline?

don't i got Indian in my bloodline?

everybody wanna be a nigga but nobody wants to be a nigger

the kids say the kid *act Black* but he white
not *white* white but white *black* like city snow
he sag   know swag like white boys know how to rap
he wear the mask   know trap music hits
shmoney in shit   he say *nigga*   get a pass
he rock Jays & Nudies   so cuties notice
he down   he get ass   in class he clown   still pass
but niggas suss   second period: *thwack*
his white face flush   red as fried baloney
he grins stupidly   throws up his fists   false
bravado   voice all vibrato   means: this nigga shook
his dukes up   looking like the great white hope
a poor man's piñata   they bust him open
hoping for gummy bears   & jellybeans

23

this poem is called Beyoncé is a white woman

hot is the new chocolate   chocolate
is the new brown   brown is the new doo-doo
doo-doo is the new shit   shiiiiit is the new
news who knew? know is the new ignorant
ignorant is the old nigger   nigga
is the new black   black is the new orange
orange you glad your black ass ain't in jail?

jail is the new plantation   plantation
is the old blues   blue is the new ivy
league   Blue Ivy is the new envy   Be
yoncé is the new body new baby
mama the new feminist airbrushed white
white is the new blood blueblood old blood beige
beige is the new rage the new whiteblack   blood

i know you are but what am i?
for Raven-Symoné

not African American either
except when being American gets
mistaken for black   for unpredictable
for gun   in the foreground   forced to the ground
for being brown   for Brown versus Board of Ed
for bullets to the forehead—for us   by us
O beautiful for spacious skies for amber
waves of grain O beautiful for faceless
cries for amber graves of pain   for African
blood that remains despite your American
claims for citizenshit—forbidden love hidden
'fore master get his whip or his dick   forced
fucks foreshadow foreplay   for jungle fever
forever remember: twas them Africans made you
formidable   unfuckwitable   lest you forget

untitled / or / niggas been ahead of they
time since the beginning of time

prehistoric afro futuristic antagonistic
ragamuffin natural mystic slapboxing pugilistic
cosmic slapstick beautiful black lips slathered in chapstick
fucking plagiarists made ya fists twist backwards blackness
is the business for those who won't witness that wackness
like: elvis's pelvic thrusts to robin thicke's marvin gaye
dicksuck—the gig's up turn graceland into quicksand ampersand
ya motherfuckin' fists up might as well slit ya wrists up
than dodge bullets homicidal Harriet's shotgun
solidified survival solidarity Harriet be
the original American idol word to ya bible
Babylon prehistoric rock pile Amiri Baraka
rocked ya chakra spearchucker sci-fi motherfucker
black like Oprah's ass & a big pot of okra—huh!

parable of the fists
after Glenn Kaino

Harriet painted a black fist on the fucking flag
sat in the principal's office fist thrust in the air
when Mama came the worried white woman
told of other instances of Harriet's graffiti:
a fist scrawled in black crayon on a poor pale
face floating in a history textbook
a rather large fist penned in black sharpie
on the back of Jake's white button-down oxford
bleeding ink tattooed the boy's freckled skin
a side panel on Margie's Hello Kitty lunchbox
& every veneered surface from chemistry to art
the school's psychologist who pried open Harriet's
composition notebook presumed abuse but Mama
said: *my child draws fists to keep from using them—*

how to be a tomboy

step 1: dress burning ritual

gather them—the pink, the frilly   girly
frail fabrics of pastel punishment—
in your puny arms   heap them in the tub
rub the bottle of bumpy face for courage
then a swig to know what your father's tongue
taste like   antiseptic of discontent
the quick burn in your throat is a good thing
tomboys should be unafraid of sting & scar

disable detectors   open all windows
liquor up the torture   all damp & limp
flick a match or two toward that pile of vile
femininity   altar of awkward & itch
you will no longer be their bobby socked bitch
sit on the toilet   light a cigarette   watch

step 2: pee-pee transitioning phase

wear the tighty-whiteys   the ones you stole
from brother's underwear drawer   finger
the magic slit in the fabric   imagine
such convenience   a penis   to point at a tree
a graffitied wall   a babydoll on fire
why are you stuck with such boring anatomy
victim of squat & wipe   peach fuzz   unripened
breasts   Thursday's panties at your ankles
this be a study in angles & physics
calisthenics of thrust   trust in the wizard
of whizz   straddle that porcelain saddle
& aim   blame no one but your mama & god
tragedy of gravity   what odd impulse this
tomboys don't pee-pee—they take a fucking piss

29

step 3: boy-bonding ceremony

throw rocks at pigeons for their attention
boys flock to the promise of blood   curse
when you miss & when your stone kisses the head
of the bird say the word *fuck* like your luck
is out to spite you   if they invite you
to the river   be cool & nod   kick a can
the whole way   lose your girlish sway for swag
fuck unicorns   your new uniform   dirt
& that faded sweatshirt with the Bruce Lee iron-on
when they pull out their dicks to piss don't flinch
wince the sunlight in your eyes & spit at the hiss
of it   then pull out that cigarette   smashed
in your ass pocket   light & spit again unabashed
slow drag   then no-look pass   the take   means you in

never could jump double dutch

is being double-handed a big butch badge?
awkward tomboy whacking wayward while
femmes wedged themselves between the great
white whoosh of wires—plan b: wait for warm
wrists to kiss mine as she whines: *nooo, like this*
meanwhile uncle Mel was on that upstate
percolate   got polaroids as proof   me:
all buck-toothed   corduroys & pro-keds
it was the 80s: cokeheads & weed seeded
on a Lionel Richie album cover
then i never thought my lover could be
woman   then i never thought i'd be shamed
of my mama—to replace her with risk & fuck

proxy

when she smiles her hand masks mouth like reflex
and like reflex my heart breaks wondering
years her smile has struggled against smother
and dishpan palm—the pink pink gums over
exposed spaces between each tooth hold place
for the missing: mama—& kissing girls
might be a not-so-subtle substitute
tomboyish & cute with lavender lip
balm & raspy voices seeking to calm
history of chatter—scatter of teeth
a smattering of laughter hides beneath
sheath of palm censoring all that ugly
noise—girls who look like boys whispering sweet
nothings mama never said: *smile, baby*

evidence of fun

after Ryan McGinley

when you mix whiskey   wine   & a woman
that fine   time blurs like rows of pines while driving
south   her mouth alone flattens me like roadkill
& i am a wide-eyed animal dodging
her every move except we don't move
so much as wind up somewhere wedged against
bathroom faucet   mirror   we see ourselves
blurring—a too fast photograph—streak of light
our fingers seek middle of the night trouble
coffee table tableau: takeout boxes
remotes   parking tickets   glasses of red wine
blur—we in bed   clueless how we got here
retracing steps with a makeshift compass:
sheer shirt   no bra   titties pointing   east   west

one day Ellen Gallagher will make paper
wigs for our wedding day

i hold all my funk in my mouth   armpit
& cooch   dyke dowry   decanter of scotch
mason jar of homemade hooch   what's your
pleasure?   scour me with lavender   lather me
in shea butter   palm roll my locs   gather my
best words into books   open your palms   let me
unlock all that you secret   a hush inside
your hands ferments to palm wine   let us drink
& lie upon a kilim woven with our fur
fingertips fiery with saffron   blue
from indigo   dyed with the beet sweet
blood of our undoing   let our ribs
be the loom   make wool of this skin   cotton
of this hair   warp & weft   love will doom
what's left of us

audition for the bed

touch   don't touch   *yellow elbow*   florescent moon
new moon   sleep   sleepless   *red eye*   snore   don't snore   slob
don't slob   hair   no hair   *brown pussycat*   hairless
boxers   no panties   *black dildo*   breath   breathless
scratch   don't scratch   rough   not rough   *pink fingernail*   hard
hardly   *ashen foot*   don't lick   lick   kiss   don't kiss
don't tell   tell   hurry-up   slow down   *dark mouth*
there   right there   not now   now   *blue kneecap*   don't dream
dream   scream   shhhh   light   no light   *golden hair*   goodnight
no night   fight   don't fight   *purple lip*   layover
no flight   flight   *green eye*   cry   don't cry   wetness   dry
don't wait   wait   flail   don't flail   *pale armpit*   handcuffs
peach thigh   dive   don't dive   drunk   drink   think   don't—

open heart

after Zara McFarlane

if the skin resembles an instrument
most likely percussive—xylophone ping
then what becomes of teeth after surgeries
guised as conversation—violin strings?
if the pores record every memory
silly sieves sucking sounds and images
then what lovers are lost in the laundry
of bedsheets   spit   armpits   fits & rages?
if the dumb clumsy hands clap and clasp
at choice vowels and vestiges of voice
then what questions remain burrowed in throats
asked lacerations stitches of white noise?
if a closed mouth is a broken door to me
then *an open heart is both a lock and key*

honeycomb

after Glenn Ligon

to suck honey from a honeycomb denotes
pleasure to suck honey from a finger
denotes an oral fixation to suck
honey from silver teaspoon denotes a
proper upbringing to suck honey from
a fist denotes a proclivity towards
a black power politic to suck
honey from a text message denotes skewed
optimism to suck honey from a
glass slipper as opposed to a flip-flop
denotes classism to suck honey from
an ice cube denotes a chill demeanor
but honey, *to save that honey in a jar*
denotes a dangerous obsession

untitled

after Glenn Ligon & Zora Neale Hurston

my tongue two-faced tongue-tied tired and—i
dunno what it be sayin half time—   feel
like shit in my mouth unfamiliar—   most
these folks don't expect it cuz—   colored
sound like blue notes not dictionaries—   when
i speak sometimes words look like flowers—   i
gotta nother voice sound like Sally—   am
silly to be bullied all proper—   thrown
into green gardens   mouthful of thorns—   against
ebonics lurking behind dull teeth—   a
weapon awaiting redemption song—   sharp
as Sunday morning   a blackness turned—   white
these wild words of mine sing in the—   background

dear Ebonics

you be a clever bitch   how you say *book*
& mean: *get the fuck outta here*   how
you say *bad* but mean: *Pam Grier*   how you roll
your eyes at Webster one minute be twerking
in his sheets the next   how you say *cracker*
ofay   honkey   & mean: *mean motherfucker*
how you bend— break— make shit up— mispronounce—
how it be cool as hooch in a house of countless drops
how your daddy *the dozens*   your mama
jive   how you conjugate & signify
simultaneous   with your machete
& alla your heart   & when whitewash tries
to render your black spectacular irrelevant
your heartbeat whisper: *i be   i be   i be*

39

something to put some thing on
after Rashid Johnson

where do chains go without an unwilling nigger?
where do gold chains go without a willing nigga?
where does the brand go without a shivering hide?
what of the whip and welt without a back?
where do we place this beastly black burden
without a body of water where goes this vessel?
this shackle gone to rust without a dusty foot
what to make of trees bearing ordinary fruit?
what good a noose without a nigger's neck?
where the flames gone shake their shimmy? no body
for nobody to climb on top of no mouth to speak of
no thing like innocence to drape semen from
nothing resembling a body or a booty
or a table—something to put some thing on

the body that i'm performing in doesn't understand limits
after Jacolby Satterwhite

barbecue teeth   meaning charred so black
it's white   Barbie thiefs the subconscious skin
knee   skim milk & silk durags   drags queen
the river neon pink & luscious   faghags
straight as cigarettes but curvy as birds
named Precious   praise what the geometry
suggests   hands masturbating circumference
what choice but succumb?   become friends
eat each other down to the white meat   what
choice but suck   cum   become dominion
of sequins   what is femininity if not
pageantry?   a pantry of days of the week
panties   which way is Tuesday?   & which is
the rudest way to say *unicorn porn*
besides this poem?

the garbage disposal ate your horoscope again

blackening—imitation plantation

instantaneous vertigo   Virgo
rising   mercury retrograde   parade

gone backwards into the black   all the stars
are merely ancestors teeth aglittering
when i say gone fishing look for the tuna tins

this skin say hooligan   insides made chitlin
noose versus the loony bin   what'll ya halve?
what'll you whole?   what you tint toward
when it count & ain't nothing but they skin

white as lint   spooking your astrology
& gangster-like logic   all your peacock
gone to chicken   all your faggot gone
to mom jeans   moonbeam white & two-faced
as any Gemini   as any Pisces coming & going at once

fool's gold or nigga please (the Ebonics remix)

                    speech so spectacular   teeth rot wit bling
                          everything from this angle smells
                        of the king &   his damned prepositions
                        determined to phrase me out—i grow fat
                        with entertainment   hairless politicos
                          make my elbows scoff with ash   & cuz
            my ancestors colored me   all the words wound
                    like song   some wrong wail   or inspired
                          gospel warbling night sky purple
                        but i am more regular than this   more
                    failure than figment   the channels of your
                          imagination you get for free—
                          this pigment be   basic cable reality

TV where a Black girl drinks too much
& thinks too   much of the time she worries
her tooth enamel beige & reads Clifton
& Lorde— which the king misinterprets
as *lawd*—*O Lord* (echoes: *oh lawd   oh lawd*)
my ancestors died preoccupied with white
jesus speeches of promised lands &
other blonde bland fairytales & when the king
said *fare thee well* i smelt a bamboozle
as fine as swine   but my eyes cataract
with such flashbacks—member when the word
was with god & the word *was* god? member
when the word became flesh & all a man

had was his word & his word
was his bond? didn't nobody care bout
the king's flaccid cursive   his breath reeking
of chitlin wine & divine adjectives
salt-cured   & retaining spit   amounts
to nothing more than shitpiles
or pretty little remnants if i am
to be polite about my whitewashed
cockney—i grow cockeyed with boredom
am prone to sudden fits of breakdance
spinning on my skull to cure the doldrums
but alas, the king hears *dull drums*
& everything blurs tribal & humid

& archaeological & obsessed
with teeth   which you already know
rot with bling so—i—last dragon like
with all my natural resources
glowing   hot & mercurial
in my mouth   resist fists white knuckling
toward some sad sequel of Tarzan
or Roots   i go all
Moms Mabley on them— stomp the yard
slack-jawed   chompers in my boots—
all them niggers get:
artifact breath   wet
with   whiffs   of   fool's   gold

acknowledgments

4 poems from this book appear in a chaplet also entitled *& more black*, published by Belladonna*, Fall 2016.

Great appreciation to the woke-ass editors who had the nerve to publish the following poems:

Beltway Poetry Quarterly: "the pornography store is closed so you will have to make your own death"

Bettering American Poetry 2015: "this poem is called Beyoncé is a white woman," "i know you are but what am i?"

Connotation Press: "self-portrait exaggerating my white features," "self-portrait exaggerating my black features"

Eleven Eleven: "this poem is called Beyoncé is a white woman," "i know you are but what am i?"

Fjords: "from here i saw what happened and i cried"

Little Patuxent Review: "honeycomb"

Muzzle Mag: "with that ass, they won't look at your eyes"

Obsidian: "people in glass towers should not imagine us," "dear ebonics," "everything out our mouth magic" (originally titled, "dear ebonics (post script)")

OCHO: A Journal of Queer Arts: "cravings," "evidence of fun," "proxy"

Sidekick Lit: "untitled (after Glenn Ligon & Zora Neal Hurston)"

Tin House: "one day Ellen Gallagher will make paper wigs for our wedding day," "the garbage disposal ate your horoscope again"

Torch Literary Arts: "you are a remarkable woman (now hurry up and die)," "something to put some thing on"

Tupelo Quarterly: "ancestors"

Winter Tangerine: "parable of the fists"

Enthusiastic thanks to the family, folks, friends and foundations that helped to make this book public and possible, especially the Cave Canem Foundation, David Gibbs, and the Face Out program at the Community of Literary Magazines and Presses (CLMP), and the Jerome Foundation. Especial gratitude to Kate Angus and Joe Pan at Augury Books who busted their humps for this book to exist. Mad love to Alexandria Smith and Chiara Bartlett for coming through with the one-two punch on the cover. So grateful to all the hands and minds that finessed these pages.

about the author

t'ai freedom ford is a New York City high school English teacher and Cave Canem Fellow. Her poetry, fiction, and essays have appeared in the *African American Review, Apogee, Bomb Magazine, Calyx, Drunken Boat, Electric Literature, Gulf Coast, Kweli, Obsidian, Poetry, Tin House,* and others. Her work has also been featured in several anthologies including *The BreakBeat Poets: New American Poetry in the Age of Hip-Hop* and *Nepantla: An Anthology Dedicated to Queer Poets of Color.* Her first collection, *how to get over,* won the 2015 To the Lighthouse Poetry Prize, published by Red Hen Press. In 2018, she won a Face Out Emerging Writers Award from the Community of Literary Magazines & Presses. t'ai lives and loves in Brooklyn, where she is an editor at *No, Dear Magazine.*